JACK BUSH ON PAPER

BY KAREN WILKIN

THE KOFFLER GALLERY
A BRANCH OF THE JEWISH COMMUNITY CENTRE, TORONTO
4588 BATHURST STREET, CITY OF NORTH YORK
METROPOLITAN TORONTO, ONTARIO, CANADA

CREDITS

COVER ILLUSTRATION & DESIGN
RENATA REALINI

TYPESETTING & PRINTING
SOMERSET GRAPHICS CO. LTD.

PHOTOGRAPHIC CREDITS
TOM MOORE – 19,20,21, 23,24,25,26,27,28,30,31,32,35,36,36,07,00,
39,40,41,42,43,44,45,46,48,52,53,55,56,57,58,59,60.
ELEANOR LAZARE – 54
HERB RAUSCHER – 50
JOHN TENNANT – 49

COLOR SEPARATIONS
PHOTRA LIMITED

EXHIBITION ITINERARY

December 3/85 – January 30/86	Koffler Gallery, Toronto, Ontario
April 27 – May 26/86	Art Gallery of Windsor, Ontario
July 5 – September 4/86	Agnes Etherington Art Centre, Queens University, Kingston, Ontario
January – February 1987	Rose Art Museum, Brandeis University, Waltham, Mass.

©The Koffler Gallery, North York, Ontario ISBN 0-920-863-07-8, 1985

CONTENTS

DIRECTOR'S ACKNOWLEDGEMENTS

Jack Bush is a pivotal figure in the development of abstract painting in Canada. While most of his major canvases have been exhibited and documented, his smaller works on paper have not. They were often purchased as quickly as they were painted and disappeared from public view into collections across the country. In assembling this exhibition, Karen Wilkin researched and borrowed paintings from public and private collections in both Canada and the U.S.A. including selected works from the Jack Bush Estate, some of which have not been exhibited before.

Karen Wilkin is a well-known curator of contemporary art, whose name has become synonymous with some of the best that has been written about the work of Jack Bush, Helen Frankenthaler and David Smith among others. Karen's essay and the photographic reproductions of the pieces provides a select overview of his paintings in watercolour and gouache from 1949 to 1975.

For conservation reasons, the number and length of time heritage works on paper are allowed to travel is limited. Therefore, this exhibition is a rare treat and it is not only an opportunity but a responsibility to document the work in colour as accurately as possible. For this accuracy we are especially indebted to the photographer Tom Moore, to Somerset Graphics and their associates, and to Renata Realini, the designer.

Through the generous and enlightened sponsorship of Corporations, Foundations and individuals such as Royal LePage Limited, The Four Seasons Hotel, Toronto, The Samuel and Saidye Bronfman Family Foundation, Mr. & Mrs. David Mirvish, Surreal Holding Inc., Arthur Silver, Nancy Hennigar, Leonard Waldman and other private individuals, exhibitions such as this are made possible. We are all indebted to Mabel Bush, his wife, Jack Bush Jr., Robert Bush and Terrence Bush for their cooperation in this venture, the Trustees of the Estate; Clement Greenberg, Kenworth Moffett, David Silcox and Aaron Milrad and to the many collectors who entrusted us with their paintings without which this exhibition would not have become a reality.

We continue to be grateful to the City of North York, the City of Metropolitan Toronto and the Ontario Arts Council, the Board of Directors, members and patrons of the Koffler Gallery and the members of the Jewish Community Centre, Toronto for their continuing support. Special thanks to the Ministry of Citizenship and Culture and International Arts Promotion Programs of the Department of External Affairs whose support made it possible for the exhibition to travel.

Last but not least, we are indebted to the President of the Gallery, Aaron Milrad, who was the catalyst that brought us all together.

JANE MAHUT

DIRECTOR, KOFFLER GALLERY

CURATOR'S ACKNOWLEDGEMENTS

I am grateful to all of the lenders to this exhibition for making their cherished works available to a larger audience. For assistance in locating works, I am indebted to Goldie Konopny, Frank Costyn and John Klintworth of Gallery One, Toronto, to Miriam Shiell of Waddington and Shiell Gallery, Toronto, to Doug Udell and Roger Woltjen of Woltjen/Udell Gallery, Edmonton, and to Alkis Klonaridis, Klonaridis, Inc., Toronto.

Thanks are due to Aaron Milrad for his help in the conception and execution of this project, and to all of the other Trustees of the Jack Bush Estate, as well, for their unflagging support and cooperation. David Mirvish supplied invaluable information and advice. Jane Mahut and the staff of the Koffler Gallery were ideal collaborators. Finally, my special thanks to Donald Clinton, for, among other things, his editing skills.

K.W. August 1985

Fig. 1
St. George Bermuda - 1934
watercolour
7¼″ ×8½″
Collection: Jack Bush Heritage Corporation Inc.

I

To say "Jack Bush" is to think of big, radiant canvases full of dazzling colour. With their unpredictable compositions and lively drawing, they are some of the most memorable pictures of the past two decades. Bush's large abstract colour paintings so dominate our sense of his achievement that it is sometimes difficult to remember that he worked in other ways as well. We forget his considerable body of works in other media: his small watercolours, his pastel sketches, his gouaches. Yet these are a significant and often pivotal part of his oeuvre.

The fact is, Bush came late to large scale painting on canvas. His first art training and his first success was with small scale works on paper. His apprenticeship as a commercial artist polished his naturally fluent and accurate drawing, and made him an accomplished painter in watercolour and gouache. Like many aspiring Canadian artists of his generation, Bush further cultivated these skills at evening art classes, producing "fine art" watercolours for his own pleasure, in his spare time, while earning his living as an advertising artist. (When he worked in oil, in these early years, he painted on the small panels that custom had decreed essential to serious Canadian landscape painting.)

Part of this preoccupation with modestly sized works and works on paper was simply practical. Bush had little money to spend on materials and his studio, for many years, was a room in his Toronto house. But he was obviously comfortable with small scale and enjoyed the capabilities of paint on paper. Well into his mature career, when he was testing the limits of his inventiveness with the big, bold paintings that established his reputation, even after he had moved into the downtown studio that allowed him to paint his largest canvases, Bush continued to make small scale works on paper.

Paper, of course, is one of the most familiar of materials. It is omnipresent in our daily lives, always at hand in its many forms, useful and disposable. A large, pristine canvas can be slightly inhibiting to the painter who approaches it; canvas implies permanence and demands that the artist produce something serious and worthy. A sheet of paper, since it is expendable and non-precious, allows the painter to feel both free to experiment and completely in control. Because of this (and because of their small size) works on paper often seem especially intimate and direct.

Fig. 2
Sun bathers - 1933
watercolour
19″ ×21″
Collection: Jack Bush Heritage
Corporation Inc.

Looking at them, we feel as if we were watching the artist at work. In Bush's pictures, this is particularly true.

What is surprising is the consistent high quality of Bush's works on paper, given their modest size. This is not to say that Bush's paintings need to bo big to he good, but they are chiefly distinguished by their marvelously varied colour and Bush's abillty lo urchcctrate hues, by setting them side by side or at telling intervals, often seems to need room in order to declare itself fully. After all, the sensation of a great deal of red against a great deal of blue is different from the sensation of small touches of the same rod and hlue.

Bush's quirky drawing, too, frequently seems to depend on sheer size, in order to be abstract. The calligraphic flourishes that underlie some of his most inventive contigurations ccace to he illusionistic simply because they have been scaled up. Instead of reading the loops and whorls as handwriting or as the complex shapes of flowers or whatever else Bush's imagery can suggest, we see only declarative, eccentrically shaped patches of colour, enlivened by the vestiges of their origins but divorced from them because of their scale. Then, too, the need to enlarge helped Bush to exorcise the fluent hand gestures of his usual drawing style from his paintings. As his work matured, Bush struggled to resist his natural facility. Eventually he succeeded in reserving "good drawing" for his commercial art, and allowing the awkward and the unexpected full play in his painting. Increasing the size of his canvases forced him to reinvent his hand gestures at a new scale, eliminating slickness and strengthening his imagery.

Yet for all their differences in actual size, the characteristics of Bush's large paintings are present in his works on paper. They seem neither miniaturized nor scaled-down. Paradoxically, they can even seem scaled-up since calligraphic elements in the paper works often occupy a larger part of the picture and are more densely packed than in the canvases where the distance between elements can be important. Both the similarities and differences between Bush's canvases and works on paper are evidence of a dialogue between all of his pictures, whatever their scale, whatever their medium.

For Bush, working on paper was not secondary to working on canvas. It was not just a respite from the physical exigencies of large scale painting, nor was it merely a way of preparing for more major works. Bush's gouaches and watercolours are intimately related to his canvases, but quite independent of them. Bush seems particularly inventive on paper, especially uninhibited, and in fact, works on paper frequently played a significant role in the development of his imagery and the evolution of his paintings. His watercolours and gouaches often anticipate notions that he later explored on canvas, or else they recapitulate and enlarge ideas that he first proposed in his paintings. The works on paper and the canvases illuminate each other.

II

From the time he first began to make serious art, Bush worked on paper. At the very beginning of his career, during the decades before his first investigations of abstraction, he painted figurative watercolours, usually landscapes or urban scenes, but also portraits, figure groups and the occasional still life. Executed in the '20s, '30s and '40s, they have a strong period flavour. Bush's way of drawing seems noticeably of its time in these works – simultaneously slick and blocky, with both the easy naturalism and the stylizations that made him such a sought after commercial artist. These early watercolours record his forays into the countryside near Toronto, his family and friends, holidays and special events. Some are straightforward enough; others verge on expressionist exaggeration. In the late '40s, just before Bush abandoned representation for his first experiments with abstraction, there is a group of simplified, symbolic pictures, often with religious themes. Bush became well known for his watercolours and exhibited them regularly in the official shows of the Canadian Society of Painters in Watercolour. He became a member in 1942, held several executive offices, including the presidency of the Society, and continued to exhibit with the Society until 1961.

With the penetration of hindsight, we can see elements of Bush's future painting in his early watercolours – characteristic configurations, ways of juxtaposing colours, typical "Bush" shapes. He seemed to seek the shapes we now recognize as "his" in nature, just as he sought subjects that provided him with "excuses" for the kind of varied, intense colour we associate with his developed painting. All of this helps Bush's early work to look quite different from that of his colleagues, including the artists who set the standard for English Canada at the time, the sacred cows of landscape painting,

Fig. 3
The prophet - 1947
watercolour
30¼″ ×22¾″
Collection: Jack Bush Heritage
Corporation Inc.

the Group of Seven. Well into the 1940s, their scenes of unpopulated wilderness, thickly brushed and flatly patterned, remained a benchmark for younger artists. Bush liked to reminisce about how worried he had been, as a young man, by his inability to make paintings like those of the Group. "They kept coming out like Bush," he said, Only later did he realize that that independence was an advantage.

His own predilection for eccentric, floating shapes and unexpected juxtapositions of colour continued to assert itself, and by the late '40s, near abstract shapes had begun to dominate his watercolours, all but eclipsing the naturalistic images that had sparked the pictures in the first place. Seen in retrospect, the watercolours of this period seem to prefigure what we now recognize as Bush's developed style because of their detached shapes, their limpid colour and their clarity. Sometimes, they look like early Bush overlaid with late Bush. The impulse towards abstraction is there, but it seems as though Bush did not trust it, as though he needed the reassurance of some justification in actuality.

He retained this throughout much of his life as an artist, no matter how abstract his work became. Some of his most startling and successful images, some of his most inventive formats, were triggered by his experience of every day things: his garden, patterns on carpets or wallpaper, his friends' clothing, shop windows. Except for the **Stripe** pictures of 1967, it wasn't until his last series, the **Totems** and the "floating stroke" pictures with musical titles, that Bush seemed willing to rely more completely on his ability to invent, but even then there are flashes of his old way of leaning on the commonplace as the starting point for inspired departure.

Whatever the spark that provoked the invented image, Bush was painting without **obvious** references to observed reality by the early 1950s. This dedication to abstraction set him apart from the majority of painters in English Canada. In Montreal, abstraction had flourished since the early 1940s, first in the expressionist works of **Les Automatistes** and later in the planar geometry of **Les Plasticiens**, but both movements were contained within French Canada. The handful of Toronto painters interested in abstraction – including Bush – banded together to exhibit as Painters Eleven in 1953, and despite the radicalness of their art (by Toronto standards) began to enjoy a certain success.[1]

Bush's canvases of the 1950s were strongly influenced by

contemporary New York painting. He admired the apparently spontaneous, worked look of orthodox Abstract Expressionism and like his New York mentors, strove to allow all states of a painting's evolution to remain visible in the finished picture. The works he showed with Painters Eleven had the density and layering of a devoted follower of de Kooning. They are obviously deeply felt and ambitious paintings, but they often seem clotted and congested. The transparent colour and lucid shapes of earlier works are obscured by repeated layers of strokes and dramatic accenting with darks. Bush's watercolours and coloured ink drawings of the time are no less deeply felt, no less dramatic than the canvases, but they are far more simpler, less layered and as a result, clearer and more successful.

Clement Greenberg's now famous 1957 trip to Toronto to visit the studios of most of the members of Painters Eleven[2] provoked, as it is rumoured, the next major change in Bush's art. It led to a turning point in his career, although not in the way that Bush's detractors like to insist. The anti-Bush faction maintains that Greenberg told Bush what to paint and then masterminded his sucess. Any artist whose studio Greenberg has been in know the absurdity of the first claim, and as to the second, it was nearly fifteen years after Greenberg's first visit before Bush's paintings began to sell with any regularity. The visit **was** the beginning of a close friendship that lasted until Bush's death in 1977. Although Greenberg, in time, became a valued visitor whose opinion Bush sought, he was far from enthusiastic about the paintings he saw on his first trip. He found them mannered and derivative. Of everything he saw in the studio, he was most interested in the small watercolours: these very likely included the **Oscar's Death** series, made the previous year as Bush's way of mourning his friend and colleague in Painters Eleven, Oscar Cahen, who had been killed in an automobile accident. Greenberg's only recommendation to Bush was that he make his large paintings the way he made his small watercolours.

Bush was doubtful about the idea and even more doubtful when he tried to paint economically and directly on a large scale. He disliked the results, finding them "too simple," and returned to his dense, layered method. Before long, though, he found he was becoming more and more unhappy with his canvases. The only ones that held his attention, that continued to challenge and puzzle him, were the "too simple" pictures derived from his watercolours. The rest is familiar. What we now acclaim as Bush's distinctive way of painting dates from this time; his works on paper pointed the way.

Bush continued to work on paper a good deal during the first years that he painted in his new, stripped-down manner. It was a comfortable link with his earlier ways of working and no doubt gave him courage, when he was about to tackle a large, expensive canvas. That reassurance, the security of having successfully worked out a similar (but not identical) picture at a smaller scale, must have been particularly welcome, since Bush's method of direct painting allowed little or no reworking. If he did not get it right the first time, there was almost nothing that could be done to salvage the picture. Bush did manage to turn a certain amount of overpainting – usually cancellation of an image with a colour almost the same as its surroundings – into a virtue. As in Adolph Gottlieb's **Bursts**, which Bush knew and admired, the resulting halo of subtle colour helped anchor the shape to the ground, creating an enriching inflection. Nevertheless, this was not something that could be done often, or in all parts of a painting.

One of Bush's first major series, the **Thrusts** of 1961 (which owe something to Gottlieb in their opposition of contained and expanding shapes) developed slowly, from images first suggested in watercolours of the late '50s. Stylized tree stumps, among other things, anticipate the shape of the developed **Thrusts**. A watercolour of 1960, **Blue Thrust on Yellow**, (present whereabouts unknown) was the first simplified version of the motif, which Bush treated with increasing audacity in the **Late Summer** series of 1961. The first **Thrusts** on canvas, exhibited in Bush's first one man show in New York, at Robert Elkon Gallery in 1962, were begun after the paper versions and expand the possibilities of the configuration even further.

Bush spent the month of October 1962 in New York, staying at the Chelsea Hotel. He painted approximately twenty-five gouaches there, some of which furnished the images that he would pursue on canvas for the next several years. The **Chelsea Hotel** series includes the genesis of the stacked, pinched **Sash** format, for example. The **Sashes** themselves and their variations, **Columns** and **Fringes**, absorbed Bush's attention until the late '60s, chiefly on canvas, but he also investigated these formats on paper[3] The gouache versions of the **Sashes** and **Columns** are not simply reductions of the ideas explored elsewhere at a larger scale. They tend to be sparer, so that each band of colour is forced to carry more visual weight, each

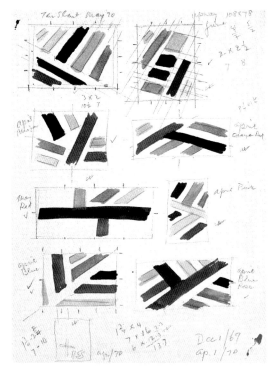

Fig. 4
Sketches for series D - 1969
pencil and felt pen
12″ ×8¾″   Collection: Jack Bush Estate

Fig. 5
Sketch for concerto for two violins - 1976
pencil and chalk
5⅙″ ×7″   Collection: Jack Bush Estate

nuance is forced to become more eloquent.

The apparent spontaneity of Bush's work notwithstanding, there is evidence of careful preparation or at least, of hard thinking about his motifs, even before he attempted them at a modest scale. From the early '60's on, Bush made tiny colour trials and studies, some no more than a few inches square, whenever he could, on whatever came to hand. It is possible that he began this practice even earlier, but the first that have survived, found in his studio after his death, are **Sashes** and **Sash** variations. These rapid studies exist on pages torn from the memo pads of the advertising agencies where Bush worked, on envelopes, writing paper, paper napkins, hospital menu cards, note pads. Bush seems to have made them anywhere – riding the subway, watching television, waiting for appointments. Felt tip markers in a range of brilliant colours had just become widely available and Bush loved them. They made bright, transparent sweeps of colour, miniature equivalents of his scaled-up brush strokes and bands of colour. They even bled a little, as paint on canvas did. Bust tried hundreds of possibilities with these coloured markers, revelling in their portability, their neatness and their intensity. He made other sketches, almost as lively, in pencil alone, as trials of placement and shape.

Bush continued to dash off these lilliputian studies for the rest of his life. He had an uncanny ability to translate these tiny sketches into large scale paintings, without losing any of the vitality of the original notion, and he developed many of the small notations into major canvases. It goes without saying that this was not a process of slavish, mechanical enlargement, any more than it had been when Bush first attempted to make large paintings like his watercolours of the 1950s. Like any good painter, Bush was attentive to the painting's demands and alert to the suggestions that arose in the course of working. The issue is slightly confused by Bush's habit of using the sketches both as trials for future possibilities and as records of the paintings realized from them, especially towards the end of his life.

In the 1970s, Bush began to make his small studies in coloured chalk rather than in felt pen. Perhaps he felt that the grainy chalk better approximated the surface of his '70s paintings, just as the smooth, bright markers had mimicked his earlier canvases. The chalk studies were drawn in groups, on the backs of letters or writing paper, then cut apart into single images and pinned to the studio wall, to serve as suggestions for paintings. After a canvas had been successfully derived from the original small notation, Bush would correct the working sketch to make it correspond exactly to the finished painting. He then added the date of completion, measurements and the eventual title; some sketches have two dates – that of the sketch and that of the finished canvas. Charming as these coloured notes are and helpful as they may bc in giving us a sense of Bush's working methods, they are simply studies. Bush never intended them to be exhibited. He preserved them only as records of the pictures that they generated.

During the late '60s and '70s, Bush's production of large scale paintings greatly increased. He was working, after 1966, in a good sized studio on Wolseley Street, in later years with an assistant to help with studio chores. In 1968, he had at last given up his advertising work to paint full time. Bush was always proud of his success as a commercial artist; he became art director of several well known Toronto agencies, including his own, Wookey, Bush and Winter. He maintained that he was good at it, that it had allowed him to support his wife and sons well, and that since he earned his living in a world apart from his painting, it had freed him to make his art exactly as he pleased. Nonetheless, he was obviously delighted to be able to devote himself to painting. The sheer amount of work from his last years is a good indicator of how Bush spent his time, and his success rate was higher. Not only did he make more pictures, but he felt compelled to destroy fewer. He painted and kept more pictures just in 1974, for example, than he had in all the years between 1961 and 1964.

Although Bush worked principally on canvas after leaving the advertising world, he also devoted several brief, but intense periods to work on paper, a series of uninhibited campaigns at smaller scale. The first of these in 1969, was prompted when Bush was hospitalized with a severe attack of angina and underwent a series of heart function tests. Characteristically, he focussed his attention on the visual phenomena of cardiac technology, and as soon as he was back in the studio, the jagged lines of the electrocardiogram and the blips of the monitor found their way into a series of gouaches. He later said that the floating sharp-edged shapes of these pictures were how he visualized his pain, but the shapes had existed overtly in his painting for almost a decade and in disguised forms for longer than that. They are typical "Bush" configurations, part of his visual language, quite apart from their associations with discomfort and fear.

Not only was Bush able to translate a disturbing experience into a visual metaphor that was familiar to him and therefore, perhaps comforting, but he was able to use that metaphor in playful, sparkling pictures that seem completely unrelated to the experience that provoked them. The **Spasm** series of gouaches has no hospital connotations, no matter what suggested them. The series is looser and more slapdash than any of Bush's canvases of the period, indeed than most of Bush's other works on paper. The pulsing lines, angular shapes and pale, saturated colours are set free and intensified by their white grounds. The canvases that use these images, which followed the gouaches, are equally fresh, clear and lively, but they are somewhat smoother and slightly less immediate.

In the 1970s, the relationship of Bush's canvases and works on paper changed. The gouaches no longer necessarily preceeded the paintings. It is often difficult to determine which came first – despite Bush's meticulous dating and careful records – simply because his concerns are identical, whatever his medium. He was in full command of his unmistakeable visual vocabulary, using with equal freedom images extracted from his idiosyncratic perceptions of the world around him and images derived from his delight in his materials. Whether Bush is working on paper or on canvas, his language remains the same, in the works of the '70s. The differences that result from his reponse to the particularities of scale and medium become all the more telling because of this.

For example, from September through November of 1970, Bush painted a large group of gouaches that develop more fully the geometric bar and loop figures present in canvases made earlier that year. Like the canvases, the gouaches oppose geometric and non-geometric shapes, deployed in sizzling colours against mottled grounds. For all their similarity, the paper works are both freer and more concentrated than the paintings they echo. In the large scale paintings, we are first struck by the contrast of major elements: the large divisions of the picture, the play of coloured figure against coloured ground. On paper, we are more concerned with the physical intricacies of each work. Their small size draws us close, so that we are particularly aware of small variations of edge and surface, of eccentricities and deliberate awkwardnesses of drawing. In the large scale paintings, the details are at first subsumed by our sense, of the whole. On paper, the subtlest nuance becomes significant.

Colour, in the gouaches, appears to be slightly more theoretical, or at least closer to primaries, than in the canvases, as though the greater emphasis on incident demanded simplifications of hue.

Bush painted relatively little during the winter of 1970-71 and then only on canvas. But in the spring of 1971, he again began working full out, on paper, in a burst of energy celebrating his pleasure in the end of winter and the return of the flowers, leaves and colour to Toronto. The motifs of these gouaches became the basis for an equally impressive series of canvases painted in 1971 and '72.

Bush's garden had often served him as a source of colour and shapes, even long after he had stopped painting naturalistically. In 1960, when he had been painting abstractly for about a decade, he made six remarkable canvases, with "garden" motifs, including **Snowball, Peony And Iris, Bouganvillea And Flowers in a Vase**. With their glowing, translucent colour and soft-edged shapes, they are some of the most beautiful and evocative of Bush's paintings, but he exhibited none of them until his retrospective, just before his death. Perhaps he felt they were not abstract enough (wrongly, as it turns out) since he abandoned the series in order to concentrate on the **Thrusts**. Ironically, the **Thrusts** seem to have been derived from, among other things, earlier paintings of a long stemmed rose. Bush returned to the garden motif as "specifically" as he had in the 1960 pictures in the astonishing **Lilac** of 1966, which like the earlier paintings was probably triggered by his actual experience of his much-loved garden. Here the impetus appears to have been a blooming lilac tree seen through a window. Yet the painting, like the 1960 works and like the later **Spasm** pictures, translates perceptions into abstract, disembodied, coloured shapes.

Nonetheless, in both the 1960 and 1966 garden pictures, the character of the shapes is still that of the actual objects that sparked them, no matter how freely Bush extrapolated. In the "garden gouaches" of 1971, he seems to have invented a new range of non-specific but potent shapes. The exhuberant white scribble of **Apple Blossom Burst**, for example, takes more liberties with actuality than do the scattered lavender ovals of **Lilac**, good as it is, or the floating white spots of **Snowball, Peony And Iris**, good as it is. The garden gouaches are among Bush's most abstract, for all their having been inspired by something he cared about passionately, and they point the way to the superb series of his last years.

These include the **Totems** with their stacks of ragged colour

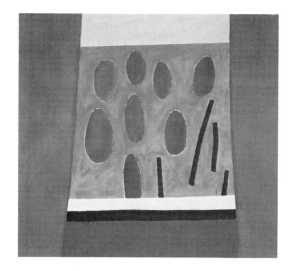

Fig. 6
Lilac - 1966
acrylic on canvas
81″ ×87″
Collection: Mr. & Mrs. David Mirvish

blocks, like loose equivalents of the earlier **Sashes**, and the "floating stroke" and "fluttering kerchief" pictures with musical titles. These series allowed Bush to unleash his full ability to use many different colours side by side, in rich, symphonic density. The musical analogy is not merely a device. Bush was a jazz enthusiast and an accomplished jazz pianist. While the musical titles of his last series were inspired by one of his sons' giving him a dictionary of musical terms, there are indications in his drawings that he was seeking some kind of equivalency between sound, colour and placement in these paintings. Whatever the motivating theory, however, the late pictures are among Bush's finest and most colouristically complex.

Bush appeared to be completely at ease with large scale and with direct painting in the late pictures. He went from tiny chalk sketch to eight foot canvas without any intermediate steps and without any loss of intensity. Except for the sketches, working on paper seems to have become less necessary to him. There are few **Totem** gouaches, for example, which is particularly noticeable in comparison with the large number of works on paper from the preceeding years. The most ambitious **Totem** gouaches were done for a poster commissioned by New York's Lincoln Center, for a Mostly Mozart concert series. Bush did three full sized trials for the poster, in order to select the one he liked best, using the same imagery that he was exploring on canvas. Bush's last works on paper, four gouaches painted in November 1975 and never exhibited, investigate both the images that were preoccupying him on canvas, at the moment, and an earlier **Totem** configuration. In a sense, they are not unrelated; the late "floating stroke" paintings could be described as **Totems** blown apart and, in fact, the first versions of the "floating stroke" pictures, the **London** series, were painted concurrently with many of the **Totems**. Bush's last gouaches make the interrelatedness of the motifs more apparent. Once again, the works on paper seem more delicate and more economical than their canvas equivalents, with Bush making his characteristic adjustments appropriate to the reduced scale of the gouaches.

III

This exhibition is not a complete retrospective. It begins not with Bush's earliest works on paper, but with a typical, if outstanding, watercolour of 1949, **Road to Orillia** An exhaustive study of Bush's early figurative pictures, their development and their relationship to the work of his Canadian contemporaries, has yet to be done. Dennis Reid's chapter on Bush's early career, ''Jack Bush: The Development of a Canadian Painter,'' in **Jack Bush**, published by McClelland and Stewart, 1984, is the first serious discussion of this period; his forthcoming exhibition and catalogue of Bush's early work, planned for the Art Gallery of Ontario, Toronto, will expand that essay.

It is logical to begin with the 1949 picture, since it marks the moment when Bush's distinctive imagery began to assert itself at the expense of naturalism, signalling the beginning of his mature concerns. This exhibition focusses on the evolution of those concerns, illustrating them with works that document Bush's development: abstract watercolours of the 1950's, including some of the **Oscar's Death** series, early **Thrust** watercolours, **Chelsea Hotel** gouaches, **Sashes, Garden** and **Totem** images, and the four last works on paper from 1975. Many of these are pictures Bush set special store by, if we can judge by his having exhibited them in the annual shows of the Canadian Society of Painters in Watercolour.

The sketches and working studies have been excluded both because Bush never intended them to be exhibited and because of their extreme fragility. They have been discussed in some detail by Duncan Macmillan, in his catalogue of an exhibition seen at the Edinburgh Festival and in London in 1980, **Jack Bush Painting and Drawings 1955-1976.** and in a related essay, ''The Red Barn: The Search for a Formal Language,'' in **Jack Bush**.

Apart from the omission of early works outside the scope of this exhibit and of working studies too perishable to be exposed to light, this exhibition affords us a coherent sense of Bush's entire oeuvre. His special gifts are evident in these uninhibited, spontaneous watercolours and gouaches: his extraordinary sense of colour, his generous drawing, his odd and engaging approach to structure. But in addition to their obvious merits, Bush's works on paper provide us with an additional benefit – an illusion of privileged intimacy. The paper works are so direct and energetic that we feel we are looking over the artist's shoulder, watching him think. That is a pleasure in itself and can only help us to see all of Bush's work better.

Karen Wilkin
Toronto
August 1985

Notes: See Page 61

• Construction with Red
1954
watercolour on illustration
board
39¾″×29¾″
Courtesy:
Allan J. Walters, M.D.

• November #10 - 1956
watercolour
15⅛″×22½″
Courtesy: Jack Bush Heritage Corporation Inc.

• November #15 - 1956
watercolour
26″×20¾″
Courtesy: Jack Bush Heritage Corporation Inc.

• November #24 - 1956
watercolour on illustration board
11″×15″
Courtesy: The Robert McLaughlin Gallery, Oshawa

23

• Separate Worlds - 1960
watercolour
25″×34″
Courtesy: Jack Bush Estate

• Late Summer #2 - 1961
gouache and watercolour
40″×30″
Courtesy: Jack Bush Heritage
Corporation Inc.

• Black Flame - 1962
gouache
35″×23″
Courtesy: Jack Bush Estate

• Dance - 1962
gouache
35"×23"
Courtesy: Mr. & Mrs. David Mirvish

• Awkward Action - 1970
gouache
30″×22½″
Courtesy:
Mr. & Mrs. David Mirvish

• Apple Blossom Burst - 1971
gouache
22½″×30″
Courtesy: Mr. & Mrs. David Mirvish

• Road to Orillia - 1949
watercolour
16¾″×33¾″
Courtesy: Corporate Art Collection
Alcan Smelters & Chemicals Ltd.

• Red Sky, White Suns - 1952
  watercolour
  13¾″×17⅝″
  Courtesy: Jack Bush Heritage Corporation Inc.

• Summer Day - 1952
watercolour and pencil
18½″×25¾″
Courtesy: Allan J. Walters, M.D.

32

Storm #2 - 1958
watercolour
30″×40″
Courtesy: Jack Bush Heritage Corporation Inc.

• Swirl - 1960
  watercolour
  26½″×20½″
  Courtesy:
  Jack Bush Heritage
  Corporation Inc.

34

• Four in Summer - 1960
watercolour
20½″×26″
Courtesy: The Art Gallery of Ontario

• White and Orange - 1961
watercolour
12½″×17⅛″
Private Collection

• Blue Moon and Sun - 1961
  Watercolour
  15¼″×21″
  Private Collection

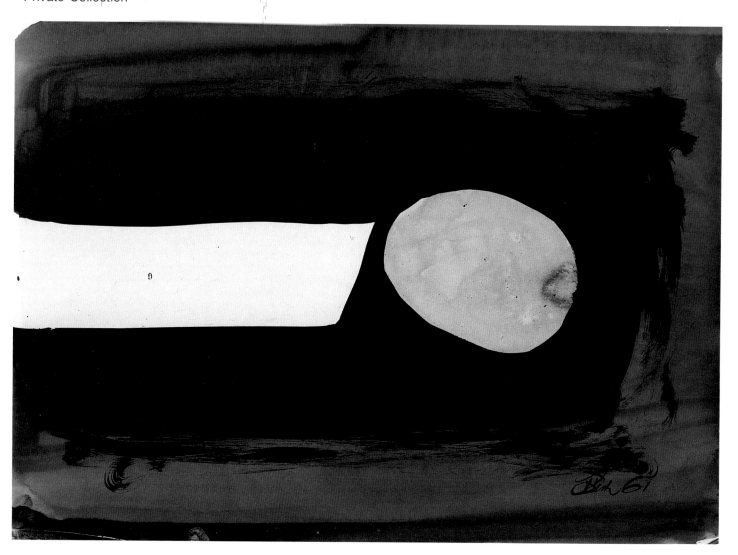

• Late Summer #1 - 1961
  gouache
  59½″×39½″
  Courtesy: Mr. & Mrs. David Mirvish

• Late Summer #3 - 1961
gouache and watercolour
25½″×34″
Courtesy: Jack Bush Heritage Corporation Inc.

• White on Brown - 1961
watercolour
15″×19½″
Courtesy: Jack Bush Heritage Corporation Inc.

• On The Way Back From Washington
1962
gouache
35″×23″
Courtesy: Mr. & Mrs. David Mirvish

41

• Pink, Green, Blue - 1965
gouache
40¾"×26½"
Courtesy: K.M. Graham

• Nice Pink - 1965
gouache
30″×22″
Courtesy: Mr. & Mrs. David Mirvish

• Untitled - 1965
  gouache
  28½″×22½″
  Collection: Alkis P. Klonaridis

• Green, Blue Plus Some Red
1966
gouache
30¼″×22½″
Courtesy: William A. Thorsell

- Spasm #5 - 1969
  gouache
  29″×22″
  Private Collection

• Flip - 1969
gouache
18½″×39½″
Courtesy: Dr. & Mrs. Robert Nadel

• Test - 1970
gouache
29½″×22¾″
Courtesy:
Miss Marla Milrad

48

• 3 Across, 3 Up - 1970
gouache
30″×22½″
Courtesy:
Mr. & Mrs. David Mirvish

● Yellow to Red Scribble - 1970
gouache
22½″×30″
Private Collection

• Blossoms Low - 1971
gouache
22½″×30″
Courtesy: Mr. Glen Cumming

• Drifting Blossoms - 1971
gouache
30″×22½″
Courtesy: Mr. & Mrs. Lewis Cabot

• Forsythia - 1971
gouache
30″×22½″
Courtesy:
Mr. & Mrs. David Mirvish

53

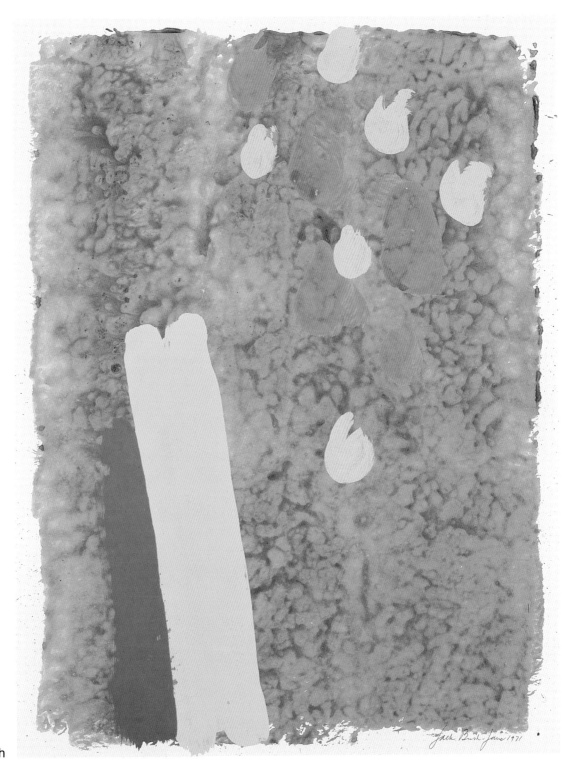

• Falling Blossoms - 1971
  gouache
  30″×22″
  Courtesy:
  Mr. & Mrs. David Mirvish

• Poster for Lincoln Centre -
  Green Arc - 1974
  gouache
  40″×26″
  Courtesy: Graham Peacock

• Pink Moon - 1974
gouache
30″×22½″
Private Collection

• Takeoff - 1974
gouache
30″×22½″
Courtesy: Mr. & Mrs. Daniel E. K

• Red and Green - 1975
gouache on Arches paper
30″×22½″
Courtesy: Jack Bush Inc.

• Pink Spoon - 1975
gouache on Arches paper
22½″×30″
Courtesy: Jack Bush Inc.

• Rockabye - 1975
gouache on Arches paper
30″×22½″
Courtesy: Jack Bush Inc.

• Zoom Down - 1975
gouache on Arches paper
22½″×30″
Courtesy: Jack Bush Inc.

NOTES:

1. The first exhibition of what was to become Painters Eleven was held in October 1953 at the Robert Simpson Company, as part of a furniture display. ''Abstracts at Home'' included paintings by Bush, Oscar Cahen, Tom Hodgson, Alexandra Luke, Ray Mead, Kazuo Nakemura and William Ronald. Later that year, Jock Macdonald, Harold Town, Walter Yarwood and Hortense Gordon joined the group. Painters Eleven continued to exhibit together until 1959.

2. Painters Eleven sponsored Greenberg's visit. Harold Town and Walter Yarwood were opposed and refused to participate. Greenberg visited the other artists, spending half a day with each.

3. Five of these formed the basis of a portfolio of five silkscreen prints, published in an edition of 100 by David Mirvish in 1965.

   Two more portfolios of five prints each, in editions of 100, were published by Waddington Galleries in 1971 and 1974. The 1971 portfolio was based on gouaches of 1970, the 1974 on gouaches of 1974. In addition to these Bush's Lincoln Center poster image of 1974 was issued as a limited edition print, and a painting of 1976, **Jetê en l'air** became the basis of a print issued for the benefit of the National Ballet of Canada this constitutes the majority of Bush's graphic work. These graphic works have been excluded from this exhibition, which concentrates on unique works on paper only.

Jack Bush   Born, Toronto, Ontario, 20 March, 1909
                  Died, Toronto, Ontario, 24 January, 1977

Selected Bibliography:

Terry Fenton   **Jack Bush: A Retrospective,** Art Gallery of Ontario, Toronto, 1976.

Duncan Macmillan   **Jack Bush, Painting and Drawings 1955-1976,** Talbot Rice Art Centre, University of Edinburgh, in association with the Edinburgh Festival, Edinburgh, 1980.

Joan Murray and Jennifer C. Watson **Painters Eleven in Retrospect,** Robert McLaughlin Gallery, Oshawa, Ontario, 1979.

Karen Wilkin, contributing editor **Jack Bush,** McClelland and Stewart, Toronto, 1984.

For a complete chronology and bibliography, see **Jack Bush**, contributing editor, Karen Wilkin, McClelland and Stewart, Toronto, 1984.

LIST OF WORKS

- Road to Orillia - 1949
  watercolour
  16¾"×33¾"
  Courtesy: Corporate Art Collection
  Alcan Smelters & Chemicals Ltd.

- Red Sky, White Suns - 1952
  watercolour
  13¾"×17⅝"
  Courtesy: Jack Bush Heritage Corporation Inc.

- Summer Day - 1952
  watercolour and pencil
  18½"×25¾"
  Courtesy: Allan J. Walters, M.D.

- Construction with Red - 1954
  watercolour on illustration board
  39¾"×29¾"
  Courtesy: Allan J. Walters, M.D.

- November #10 - 1956
  watercolour
  15⅛"×22½"
  Courtesy: Jack Bush Heritage Corporation Inc.

- November #15 - 1956
  watercolour
  26"×20¾"
  Courtesy: Jack Bush Heritage Corporation Inc.

- November #24 - 1956
  watercolour on illustration board
  11"×15"
  Courtesy: The Robert McLaughlin Gallery, Oshawa

- Storm #2 - 1958
  watercolour
  30"×40"
  Courtesy: Jack Bush Heritage Corporation Inc.

- Swirl - 1960
  watercolour
  26½"×20½"
  Courtesy: Jack Bush Heritage Corporation Inc.

- Separate Worlds - 1960
  watercolour
  25"×34"
  Courtesy: Jack Bush Estate

- Four in Summer - 1960
  watercolour
  20½"×26"
  Courtesy: The Art Gallery of Ontario

- White and Orange - 1961
  watercolour
  12½"×17⅛"
  Private Collection

- Blue Moon and Sun - 1961
  watercolour
  15¼"×21"
  Private Collection

- Late Summer #1 - 1961
  gouache
  59½"×39½"
  Courtesy: Mr. & Mrs. David Mirvish

- Late Summer #2 - 1961
  gouache and watercolour
  40"×30"
  Courtesy: Jack Bush Heritage Corporation Inc.

- Late Summer #3 - 1961
  gouache and watercolour
  25½"×34"
  Courtesy: Jack Bush Heritage Corporation Inc.

- White on Brown - 1961
  watercolour
  15"×19½"
  Courtesy: Jack Bush Heritage Corporation Inc.

- Black Flame - 1962
  gouache
  35"×23"
  Courtesy: Jack Bush Estate

- Dance - 1962
  gouache
  35"×23"
  Courtesy: Mr. & Mrs. David Mirvish

- On The Way Back From Washington - 1962
  gouache
  35"×23"
  Courtesy: Mr. & Mrs. David Mirvish

- Pink, Green, Blue - 1965
  gouache
  40¾"×26½"
  Courtesy: K.M. Graham

- Nice Pink - 1965
  gouache
  30"×22"
  Courtesy: Mr. & Mrs. David Mirvish

- Untitled - 1965
  gouache
  28½″×22½″
  Courtesy: Alkis P. Klonaridis

- Green, Blue Plus Some Red - 1966
  gouache
  30¼″×22½″
  Courtesy: William A. Thorsell

- Spasm #5 - 1969
  gouache
  29″×22″
  Private Collection

- Flip - 1969
  gouache
  18½″×39½″
  Courtesy: Dr. & Mrs. Robert Nadel

- Test - 1970
  gouache
  29½″×22¾″
  Courtesy: Miss Marla Milrad

- 3 Across, 3 Up - 1970
  gouache
  30″×22½″
  Courtesy: Mr. & Mrs. David Mirvish

- Awkward Action - 1970
  gouache
  30″×22½″
  Courtesy: Mr. & Mrs. David Mirvish

- Yellow to Red Scribble - 1970
  gouache
  22½″×30″
  Private Collection

- Apple Blossom Burst - 1971
  gouache
  22½″×30″
  Courtesy: Mr. & Mrs. David Mirvish

- Blossoms Low - 1971
  gouache
  22½″×30″
  Courtesy: Mr. Glen Cumming

- Drifting Blossoms - 1971
  gouache
  30″×22½″
  Courtesy: Mr. & Mrs. Lewis Cabot

- Forsythia - 1971
  gouache
  30″×22½″
  Courtesy: Mr. & Mrs. David Mirvish

- Falling Blossoms - 1971
  gouache
  30″×22″
  Courtesy: Mr. & Mrs. David Mirvish

- Poster for Lincoln Centre - Green Arc - 1974
  gouache
  40″×26″
  Courtesy: Graham Peacock

- Pink Moon - 1974
  gouache
  30″×22½″
  Private Collection

- Takeoff - 1974
  gouache
  30″×22½″
  Courtesy: Mr. & Mrs. Daniel E. Kert

- Red and Green - 1975
  gouache on Arches paper
  30″×22½″
  Courtesy: Jack Bush Inc.

- Pink Spoon - 1975
  gouache on Arches paper
  22½″×30″
  Courtesy: Jack Bush Inc.

- Rockabye - 1975
  gouache on Arches paper
  30″×22½″
  Courtesy: Jack Bush Inc.

- Zoom Down - 1975
  gouache on Arches paper
  22½″×30″
  Courtesy: Jack Bush Inc.